John's
Gift of Peace

Also by John T. Mudd:
Everything You Wished You
Learned In High School
Available at www.amazon.com
and other retailers

John's Gift of Peace

A collection of prayers with a common theme of peace authored by the Holy Spirit through John T. Mudd

Steel Bridge Press

Dedication

To Mom and Dad,

      I can't tell you how much I appreciate all you have done for me. I hope someday I will be able to make you proud of me. You have been the best friends and parents a guy could ever have. I may be far in distance but I hold you close in Spirit always.

All my love, John

Dear Annie, (mom)

      I just wanted to say how proud I am of you. You are the most special gift that God has bestowed upon me. You chose the best father for me that anyone could ask for. My brother and sisters are considered my best friends because of how we were raised. Thank you for all of the prayers said for me, I feel every one of them.

I love you, John

For Buddy
(dad)

You are the core of my life. O God, bless my father with the gift of peace. Allow him to feel the appreciation that I have for all that he has done for me. Reward him for his generous deeds and provide him with abundant health. Establish in me the wisdom, honesty and generosity that are the foundation of his being. Allow him to live in the comfort of Your presence with the undying knowledge of my love.

Contents

Preface

On September 11, 2001, terrorists attacked the United States. This was a life-changing event. People started praying like never before.

John Mudd wanted to do his part for his country and the world. He developed a website called Pray for Peace.com that reached everyone via email. Two prayers were sent out daily and were translated in the languages of more than one hundred countries. His mission statement on his website read:

Although we may feel helpless as individuals, together we have a power far greater then any evil that exists on earth. It is our belief that we can bring about world peace through universal prayer.

Everyone receiving his email was praying for peace. His intent was to have millions of voices reaching to God. One of his earlier prayers read:

When Terror Strikes

Protect us, O God and shield us from those who wish to harm us. Have mercy on the victims of this violent act and welcome them into Your

Kingdom. Bring comfort to their families and grant us Your peace. Prevent this deed from promoting the agenda of the evildoers. Do not allow fear to burden our economy or our freedom. Keep strong our respect for other religions and all of Your children. Strengthen our resolve to end all war, work for justice and to do Your will.

John spent many hours developing this website. His prayers were always so inspiring. When asked how he wrote the beautiful words, he said, "I ask the Holy Spirit what I should write, and then I wait until I get a tingling sensation through the back of my neck. It is then that the words just simply flow out as I type." His mother said she watched as the tears flowed when he realized it was not himself, but the Holy Spirit who had used John to get these words out. He was so humbled.

Later, John chose his favorite prayers and put them together into a book called *Gift of Peace*.

Foreword

A Mother's Tragedy

Ann and John

How do you cope when your world suddenly falls apart? That question has been asked of me many times since the horrible night of December 9, 2008. It seems, at times, like nothing can put it back together again. The sudden death of two of our children, within six weeks of each other, has forever changed my life and the lives of my family, but I am managing to survive with God's help.

My phone rang at 1:30 in the morning. It was my daughter-in-law, Joanie, screaming, "Ann, John's cabin is on fire and John is not out." I can still hear her voice in my head. I still repeat those dreadful words in my mind. My husband, Buddy, and I jumped out of bed, and rushed to our forty four year old son John's cabin, which was only a mile away from our home. The cabin was a landmark and had been built about 150 years ago. We could see flames and smoke leaping everywhere. I felt a sickness in my heart and a terrible gnawing in the pit of my stomach. I felt so helpless, but still had the presence of mind to call our priest to come and pray. Within minutes of our arrival, word had traveled fast and most of the family was there, praying, hoping and frantically waiting for the fire department's help. At that moment, none of us dreamed that John would not survive.

When we left that horrible scene and walked back into our home, the only thing I had to hold onto was his *Gift of Peace,* the prayers that John had written for the world. That book was a piece of John that I could hold in my hands. I stayed awake for endless hours. I did not want to go to sleep because I was too afraid I would wake up and have to face this horrible nightmare again. I just did not want to admit he was dead.

During the next few days, my husband and five surviving children had to make decisions at the worse time of our lives. We picked out a casket for John. It didn't seem real, yet on some level I knew it was very real. We were still in shock over what had happened. We planned the funeral. We chose the Scriptural readings and John's favorite hymns, "Here I Am, Lord" and "Let There Be Peace On Earth." Everyone was trying to do their part to help. We chose a prayer from his book for his funeral program:

Yesterday, Today and Tomorrow

My prayer for yesterday is that I gave enough of myself to make a difference in someone's life. My prayer for today is to realize and be grateful for all God provides. My prayer for tomorrow is to be humble enough to show compassion and kindness to all I encounter on my path and to spread a message of peace that can only begin with me.

There were endless stories about all the good he had done, how much he was loved, and how his wonderful smile would light up a room when he walked in. It was comforting to know how many people loved John. We just did not realize the enormous amount of lives he had touched. I didn't feel I had the right to grieve so much because John, in a way, belonged to everybody. It wasn't all about me. He left a great impact on the lives of many people.

I felt numb as I looked at his body in the casket, I still couldn't believe this terrible tragedy had actually taken the life of someone I cared for so deeply. John and I had a special relationship that most parents would envy. We could talk for hours about everything from cooking, illnesses, decorating, spirituality and world travel. He was truly my confidante. A son, I trusted and loved. He was always there for me. This was not how it was supposed to go. Children are supposed to bury their parents. My heart felt big and heavy and it hurt.

On the 21st of January, 6 weeks after his death, I attended morning Mass for John and had just finished breakfast when my phone rang. It was my daughter, Sally, telling me that the paramedics were taking my forty five year old daughter, Tricia, to the hospital because she had had a seizure. As we arrived at the emergency room, the hospital Chaplain was there, waiting for us. Right then we knew the news was not good. Tricia's heart had stopped for ten minutes and although it had started again, she never regained consciousness. We waited and prayed, waited and prayed. The family listened as I read Passing from John's book of prayers.

Passing

Bring peace to my loved one dear God as the end of their life nears. Comfort them as they make their way home to You. Death is the door to true peace with You and yet we approach it with fear. Wipe away all sorrow and bless us with the courage to face this part of our journey. Forgive Your child of any wrongs that they may have committed. Although I grieve the loss of my friend, I hand them over to You where they shall live with no more tears, absence of suffering and true peace. I long for the day that I too shall join You in Eternity.

Finally, as the whole family was gathered around her bed, God gently called her home. She, too, was suddenly taken from us. Sadly, there was a second funeral for which to prepare.

Tricia and John

A parent's greatest fear, losing a child, came true for me--twice. The reason I have been able to cope is because of my faith. Although I have not been spared the pain of loss, my faith journey that started at an early age has helped me to accept God's plan. Father John Corapi says, "God let's bad things happen to bring about a greater good." I believe that God gave John those prayers for a divine purpose. John and Tricia's work was finished on this earth. Through his *Gift of Peace*, I truly found my greatest consolation. I now feel that it is also a part of my mission on this earth to spread his gift.

Ann Mudd

Acknowledgements

This book was compiled by John's sister, Sally Mudd McLaughlin, on the second anniversary of his death. Shortly after he died, we discovered many more prayers that had not been included in his original book. Our family wanted to put together a complete collection of his works.

It is a very challenging task to complete someone else's vision. I know I felt him laughing with me throughout this process, and crying a few times as well. I hope now that it is finally complete, he is smiling.

John and Sally

Chapter 1

Let
There
Be
Peace
On Earth

Seeds

You are the beacon of light that shines on us all. Do not allow us to suffer from despair when we are constantly bombarded by the sounds of war. Keep us vigilant in our prayer for peace and remind us that we each have the power to bring forth change. Do not let disappointment overcome our faith, just because we see a world determined to set its own course. Although we may not see the goodness that comes from our earnest prayers, we trust that You hear us and touch the lives of those who most need to feel Your love. Allow our prayers to be the seeds of peace as we wait in hopeful expectation for the sacred harvest.

Gifts and Treasures

Great Provider, You have given the world so many gifts and treasures. Allow us to distribute them wisely so that all people may live humanely. Wipe away the selfishness that places huge burdens on large populations of people. Keep us focused on our mission of peace. Reinforce our commitment to do Your will. What have we gained if we inherit the world and lose our soul in the process? Peace is our prayer, peace is our desire and in You we shall have it. Keep safe all of Your people, especially those who are unable to accept You.

Humanitarian Workers

Great and Merciful Jesus Christ, we find our comfort in knowing Your love. Bring peace and security to those men and women who work in developing countries in order to better the lives of Your children. Make us aware of the sacrifices, dangers and commitments that these brave people make, while risking their lives on a daily basis. Hold them in the highest esteem and allow their example to be emulated by those able to share their time, talent and treasure. Instill in each of us the longing to help the needy, feed the hungry and to share Your love with those who live in the darkness of Your absence.

4

Political Refugees

Protect and comfort those who seek a better life, O God. Allow them to find peace. Our world is filled with an unequal distribution of the gifts that You have bestowed upon us. Allow us to share with those that have little. Remove all fear, prejudice and injustice from our hearts and allow us to welcome those that are enslaved by poverty and hunger. Provide safe passage for those that risk their lives as they seek freedom. If it is Your will, furnish them with courage, conviction and faith. Prevent us from dismissing these people as less than human. They are created in Your image. Bring each of us peace as we struggle to respect all of humanity.

Missionaries

Ever-living God, You have blessed us with Your love. Provide peace and protection to those who work in foreign lands to spread Your message. Allow the missionaries to carry out their work free from fear or harm. As individuals, these people sacrifice so many comforts that we take for granted. Give them the privilege of touching the hearts of people who may otherwise never have found You. Renew our respect for all those who take risk in order to improve the world.

Those Left Behind

O Jesus Christ, You know each of us by name and by every dream that we hold dear. Be close to those who wait for loved ones serving in foreign countries to bring forth peace. Have mercy on those who grieve the loss of their family members or friends because of the ravages of war. Bring comfort to those who face intense hardships caused by sickness, financial problems and loneliness as they suffer the agony of separation due to military conflicts. Be with all people who have been left behind as the rest of society marches on seemingly unaware of their pain. Grant that we may come to trust in Your power more frequently and open our hearts to the promises that You offer.

Political Leadership

Bless us God and provide guidance to all political leaders. Guide them as they make decisions that will bring about consequences for many generations to come. Open their hearts and allow them to understand that the only option is peace, the guideline for civilization. Keep them free from pride and self-promotion. Defeat the evil of rogue individuals who attempt to proclaim themselves masters of Your creation. We dream of a peace that will lead each of us to open our hearts to Your commandment to love one another. In You, all things are possible.

8

Soldier's Family

Everlasting God, I thank You for this day. Let my love for You grow with every breath that I take. I humbly ask that peace be granted to the families of soldiers. May they have peace of mind and be free from anxiety. Protect all soldiers as they perform their duties while maintaining peace and freedom. Give their parents strength and ease their worries. Keep all of us safe and out of harm's way. May Your peace protect all of us in times of danger and strife. Thank You for Your protection and Your everlasting love. Amen

Invest

O Jesus Christ, the treasure of Your love is our sacred reward. Teach us to invest in peace so that we may reap the benefits that come from justice, equality and respect. Turn our attention to promoting human right, opportunity and hope. Create an attitude of compassion among all nations regardless of their prominence and wealth. May all those who place their trust in Your promises come to know the hallowed peace that only comes from You. Be with each of us as we strive to reclaim the world that You created.

Path of Hope

The hope that You offer illuminates our path to You, O Jesus Christ. Teach us to give peace a chance. Allow us to find new ways to promote peace as something of great value – worthy of our resources, education and prayers. Guide us to a more broad understanding of how people of all nations suffer in the absence of tranquility. Expand our ability to show compassion to those who suffer because of imprisonment, and have been cast out by their fellow human beings. Bless us with the wisdom to see where justice is missing. May all those who suffer from fear, physical injury or mental-anxiety come to know the peace that You provide.

Tranquility

The world is great with Jesus Christ. Bring peace to those places where You have been shut out. Open our hearts and minds and renew us with Your love. Teach us to provide witness to those who do not know You. Release us from the snares of arrogance, egotism and self-absorption, which leave little room for You, O Jesus Christ. Allow Your compassion to be felt throughout the world so that peace may engulf our lives. Bring hope into the lives of those who have given up and bless them with the tranquility that You alone offer.

Soldiers of Peace

Bring peace to the lives of those called to protect our country, O God. May they never see the first blast of violence or war. Allow their presence to serve the greater good of peace. Have mercy on their families as they deal with worry, loneliness and concern. During this holiday season, renew our hearts and strengthen our commitment to find peaceful solutions to difficult conflicts. In You, O God, all things are possible.

Good Times and Bad

Your sacred friendship is our greatest
treasure, dear Jesus Christ. Bring peace
where sadness has taken root. Enable us to
work through You to achieve lasting harmony
among all nations. Show us the path that
leads to justice, respect and forgiveness.
Challenge us to live each day with purpose
and meaning. Push us to be committed to
Your command of love by employing the gifts
of charity, hope and faith. Make us strongly
aware of Your presence in times of need and
during times of joy. Come into the hearts of
those who deny You.

Peace be upon Them

We join today in prayer for those that suffer.
For those afflicted by war and terrorism – we
pray. For those who suffer from the burden
of poverty –we pray. For the people who are
hungry –we pray. For those who do not have
shelter –we pray. For those who are battered
by those they love –we pray. For those who
have lost hope – we pray. For those who are
about to die without knowing love –we pray.
We pray that they might find peace and that
their burden may end this day. Amen

Feed the World

Compassionate and ever-loving God, show us
how to spread Your goodness. Protect all
those who hunger. Fill them with Your spirit
and provide them with the nourishment that
they seek. Let all nations work to feed those
without food and find ways that will lead to
long-term solutions to end this misery.
Remove our complacency, so that we may
help alleviate starvation. Keep us ever mindful
that each victim is Your unique creation. May
the justice of feeding Your children be the
foundation for peace.

Illuminate

Your power radiates from within us, O Jesus
Christ. Allow Your love to shine throughout
the world and bring light to those who live in
the darkness of Your absence. Create a new
path of healing that will lead us to an
everlasting peace. Bless those who are
challenged by greed, hatred and pride with a
new sense of humility. Spread Your
compassion where we have failed to share our
treasures, illuminate the world with peace by
the fire of Your spirit that burns within all of
us.

Clouds

Happy are we who know the peace that You offer, dear Jesus Christ. Accept our love and allow us to honor You in all that we do. Free those who are enslaved by famine, poverty and isolation, that they may know the wondrous deeds that You offer. Bring justice to those who have been oppressed and have lost hope. Dispel the clouds of war, terrorism and violence that overshadow Your beautiful creation. Lift up our spirit and remain with us now and forever. Touch the hearts of our enemies and give them the comfort of Your love.

Military Children

Kind and merciful Jesus Christ, You are our only true comfort. Bless the children who will be saying goodbye to parents who are being deployed to prepare for war. Keep them safe and lessen the pains of their anxiety. Make us aware of the protection that You will provide for their mothers and fathers and return them home safely. Protect all of us from the tragedies born of nuclear, chemical and biological weapons. Hear our unending prayer that all war may be avoided and that calm shall blanket the world. Have mercy on us all.

Peace Poem

Good Morning God. How was Your night?
Were You able to rest? Was everything right?
Does the war that is brewing cause You great
sorrow? Does the fear that we spread dim
hope for tomorrow? What wondrous deeds
do You have planned for today? -A change
for the world, I hope and I pray. Show us
forgiveness and open our hearts. Teach us
respect for the world's many parts. Bring
forth justice and bring me to You. May we all
live in Peace as You ask us to do. This is my
prayer and I want You to know – In love, hope
and faith, I continue to grow.

Mission Peace

In You, O God, I have found my peace. Allow those of us who have been charged with the mission of working for peace to make progress. Do not allow us to become hopeless and accept what may seem inevitable. Provide us with opportunities to show our support for alternatives to war and keep our faith strong. Touch the hearts of those who live by the sword, so that they may learn the true joys of life.

Truth

You are the Truth, O Jesus Christ. Provide us with a true sense of what Peace would actually mean to the world and in our daily lives. Allow us to see a clear vision of the world where we actually love all people as ourselves. Would we be able to allow anyone to die of hunger, suffer from curable diseases or live without shelter? Permit us to envision a world free of the cost of defending ourselves and with a sense of security that no bomb can ever provide. Lessen our complacency regarding war and deepen our desire to live in peace.

Peace for a Day

Thank You God for the dream last night. It was something, I must say. I dreamt the world was filled with peace that lasted for a day. Laughter filled the streets and towns, and love touched hearts once broken. There were no pains or hunger, and not a mean word was spoken. Justice prevailed throughout the land, and the sound of war was mute. All fear was gone and hope was found, while friendship began to root. At the end of my dream, I wanted to ask, "What made everything this way?" I heard a voice that told me this, "You took the time to pray."

President of the United States

We ask that You protect and give strong guidance to the president of the United States during these fluid times, Dear God. We pray for the individual and for the office that he holds. Bless him with the courage to make tough decisions and give him insight into peaceful solutions to grave problems. As he represents each citizen of his country, may he act in ways, in which we can all be proud. Although we support the president, we acknowledge his humanity. Give him the skills to bring forth peace. The sweetest victory shall come from serving You.

Enemies of Peace

All Glory be to You, God and may Your mercifulness be known by all. Bring peace to those who are engaged in war. Spread justice throughout the land. Expose the enemies of peace and remove them from power. Fill the void, created by hate, with love, respect and hope. Free those, who have been oppressed, so that they may live fully in Your love. Allow our prayer for peace to be heard.

Mother Earth

Loving God, You have created a marvelous world and universe for all of Your children. Allow us to be wise caretakers of the land, the seas and the skies. Teach us to live in union with nature and allow us to use natural resources in efficient ways. Remove political and financial greed in our quest to feed our growing dependence upon Earth's precious gifts. Allow us to approach the environment with peace so that we may pass on to our children the benefits of a clean and healthy place to serve You.

Chapter 11

Let
It
Begin
With
Me

Yesterday, Today and Tomorrow

My prayer for yesterday is that I gave enough of myself to make a difference in someone's life. My prayer for today is to realize and be grateful for all God provides. My prayer for tomorrow is to be humble enough to show compassion and kindness to all I encounter on my path and to spread a message of peace that can only begin with me.

New Year's Prayer

Thank You, Jesus Christ for the many blessings that You have bestowed upon me during the past year. I am grateful for the people that You have placed into my life. Allow me to use the lessons that I have learned to make the world better in the future for those that I love and for those that I do not know. Help me to realize my highest purpose in life and to make good decisions, placing me where I may best serve You. Intercede on behalf of all Your faithful children and allow peace to shine on every person, every nation and on the entire world. Keep me committed to Your teachings, as I understand them, my resolve to seek justice and my prayer for peace. Reveal Yourself to me in every person that I encounter and increase the capacity of my heart, so that I may be able to contain my ever-increasing love for You.

Resolutions

Your are my strength, O Jesus Christ, and I shall lean on You at all times. Bring peace into my life and give me the resolve to stay committed to my New Year's resolution. Allow me to pray more frequently for the good of all people and less for the selfish desires that are within me. Allow me to be more tolerant and slower to pass judgment on those who are different from me. Prompt me to extend a giving hand before it is asked of me. Teach me to see You in all people, especially those who I fear the most. Grant me the courage to stand up for those too weak to defend themselves and the opportunity to share Your gift of love.

Tree in the Forest

Protect me God from myself. I have been blessed in an undying belief in You. Yet, I still think in terms of fear and doubt. I question my actions when I am confronted with peer pressure and laziness. I know that You are with me, in spirit and as my Master and still I suffer. Please grant me the peace that You alone offer. Please help me to overcome the pain of human rejection from Your family on Earth. May those that are confronted with insecurity be able to free themselves of fear and recognize that they are also part of Your creation. Your ways are not the same as our ways. Please help our religious leaders to accept that You alone are God and Your will shall be done accordingly. It takes many trees to create a forest. Peace.

Share

O Jesus Christ, You have granted me all that I need. It is impossible for anyone to give something that they do not possess. Allow me to share the gift of peace with those who have yet to accept it from You, so they too can pass it on. Give me the courage to live as a peacemaker and to see You in all that I encounter. Allow me to see the innocence in my most feared enemy and give them the vision to see in me, innocence as well. Reduce our reliance on military strength to manage hatred and replace it with true peace, born of love.

Use Me God

Most Holy God, I am so grateful to be part of Your creation. Use me as a tool to help others who are less fortunate. Protect those who struggle without the knowledge of Your love. Provide peace to those who have been betrayed by society and are cast out. For those that seek truth, reveal Yourself to them. For those that are consumed with anger and hate, show them kindness. Give peace to the broken hearted and everlasting joy to those that are without hope. We ask for all of these things in Your name. Amen

Poverty and Justice

God, Your mercy sustains us as we work to bring about justice throughout the world. Provide relief to those that are imprisoned by poverty. It is difficult for a mother to ask for peace while she and her children are starving. Anger gives way to the Truth, when Young men and women are faced with unemployment, lack of opportunity and rejection. Open new paths that will provide hope and allow them to find a meaningful existence that adds to their community. Show those of us, blessed with resources, the opportunities to better someone else's life. Start with me, dear God and allow Your peace to spread.

Potential

O Jesus Christ, You have blessed us with immense potential. Allow us to recognize our capacity to love, to care, to build, and to forgive. Teach us to look within ourselves to find the necessary attributes to establish peace in our hearts, our homes, our country and world. Allow us to get beyond our past issues of deprivation, abuse, greed, jealousy and revenge. Let us live in the present with heightened expectations for tomorrow. Use this generation to bring forth peace through, justice, virtue and humility. Establish Your presence within us.

Peace Hope Love

Where there is war, bring about peace. Where there is fear, bring about hope. Where there is hate, bring about love. Where there is God, bring about me.

Peace filled Heart

I am Yours God and am grateful to belong to Your family. I am filled with peace and find great comfort in the sense of belonging that I feel as I grow closer to You through prayer. I hope to spread this peace through my actions and by the example that I live. Although, I am unworthy of the gifts that You have shared with me, allow me to use them in a way that brings me closer to You. Through You, I find my worth.

Path to Peace

Dear God, I cherish the love that You offer me. As I start my day please allow me to seek the hungry, so that I may feed them. Allow me to find the thirsty, so that I may offer drink. Do not allow me to turn from those that I fear. Open my heart to those that are different from me. Allow me to become acquainted with those that are blessed with Your love, so that I may follow them into Your kingdom. Your peace is the treasure that I seek.

Our Best Life

Teach us to live our best life, O Jesus Christ, and leave this world better than when we arrived. You have blessed each of us with unlimited potential. Motivate us to seize upon life's opportunity and answer Your call to live. Instill in each person an unquenchable thirst for peace. Divert the energy and resources that are spent on war and defense to developing an atmosphere of lasting peace. Allow people to know that their uniqueness plays an integral part in Your plan. Guide us to share our time, talent and treasure with those who are in most need of Your love.

Let Them Hear Me

Allow me to spread Your message, O God, so that others may enjoy the peace that You offer. Provide me with a strong voice so that others may hear of Your love. Give me the courage to approach the unapproachable. Point me in the direction that will lead to opening the hearts of the oppressed. Give me patience as I wait for others to join me in praying for peace. Open the minds of those that doubt Your power and teach me to trust in Your ways.

Within Me

Reside within me, O Jesus Christ, and find a dwelling place in my heart. Bring peace to all people who suffer from the conflicts of inner turmoil. Establish Your presence in our lives and keep us ever aware of Your love. Although we are powerless against the storm that rages outside, permit us to find safety within. Bless all of us with health of mind and spirit, and fill our lives with hope as we long for the day of our eternal union with You.

I Can Do More

I can do more, O God. You have blessed me with an infinite amount of gifts and opportunities. Yet, I use them in ways contrary to fostering peace around me. I do not use every opportunity that You present to bring about justice and I allow fear to prevent me from doing what is right. Show me how to become a better person and allow me to be ever mindful of Your commandment to love one another. Keep me aware that the pleasures found here on Earth are only temporary. What I seek is Your eternal peace. Bless me with a clear mind, open heart and courage to do what it takes to spread Your message of Peace.

Use Me

Guide me, O God, beyond my fears, beyond my mistakes and my temptations. Allow me to serve You by accepting the challenges that You have placed before me. Provide me with courage to turn from the life that I am living and give me the insight to better Your creation. Teach me to see You in all people and prevent me from adding to the misery that the world now knows. Use me as Your voice so that others may hear of Your glory. Bring peace to all of us, especially those who are in the greatest need of Your mercy.

Shine

All glory is Yours, O Jesus Christ. Allow us to accept our brilliance, our potential and our splendor, which we have inherited as Your children. Teach us to shine beyond the shadows of self-doubt, fear and hate. Make us aware of the marvels that each individual possesses. Keep strong our determination to utilize this greatness so that we may serve the world and honor You. As we retreat from the darkness, may we live in the light of peace all the days of our lives.

Serving You

I proclaim Your wonders, O Jesus Christ and celebrate the life that has been given to me. Allow me to live a life of meaning and place me where I may best serve You. Lessen my habit of always asking You to help me, dear Jesus Christ, but allow me to help You in the things that You are doing for others. Increase my ability to forgive so that I may free myself of the sadness that prevents me from growing closer to You. Bless me with the ability to see goodness in all people and the joys of peace that it brings forth.

God is Great

God is great. I will speak the truth. I will not add to the injustice in the world. I will not live my life in fear. I will not react with violence when I am faced with the same. I will think with an open mind and not with bitterness. I will live my life as if it will lead me to Eternity. I will work and pray for peace. God is great.

Gift of Peace

Hold me God, in Your tender grasp. Let me know the peace that only You provide. Guide me to make the right decisions so that others may feel Your love. I am Your humble servant today and always. May my life be lived only to honor You and may that example be shown today and from this time forward. Help me to work for justice and equality. Allow my life to add something to Your wonderful creation. Today, please give me the courage to live as You have asked. Give me the strength to love my neighbor as You have taught. Do not allow fear or prejudice to prevent me from enjoying Your most precious gift – Peace.

From Me...Peace

Everlasting God, allow me to spread the message of peace with all those whom You place in my life today. Do not allow embarrassment and insecurity to prevent me from sharing Your love and the peace that it offers. I am such a small part of Your creation. In a small way let me bring about big changes. Bring forth the energy and wisdom to enable me to do Your will. In You, all things are possible. Amen

Foundation of Peace

Show me the way, O God, to build a
foundation for peace. Where should I begin?
Let me start with the first person that I meet
today. Keep my heart open and allow me to
believe that every person has the opportunity
to be a part of a peaceful world. Perhaps the
smile that I share, the extra time that I am able
to spend or the special effort I make toward
someone that I would normally ignore could
spark the fire of peace that will hopefully
engulf the Earth. I pray that You will allow me
to touch the right person. I will continue to
pray for peace.

Feed the Spirit

Allow me to feed my spirit on You alone, O Jesus Christ. Free me from the torments of worry and needless anxiety. Allow peace to fill my heart and radiate from me to those that I encounter. Permit me to hand over all my troubles to You, for I am powerless and rely completely upon Your compassion. Guide me to reach my greatest potential and allow me to serve You all the days of my life. Grant that I may be worthy of Your promises and that You may be proud of the life that I live.

Family Peace

You know my most intimate thoughts and
needs, O God. Allow me to be faithful to the
relationships that I have built and committed
to on this Earth. Prevent me from allowing
boredom, immaturity and financial woes to
separate me from the people that You have
placed in my life on my journey to You. Teach
me to respect the commitments that I have
made, the challenges that You have laid
before me and the opportunities that I share.
Provide peace in my family and allow me to live
my life as a testament to the love that I have
for You.

End Oppression

I am Your humble servant God and all good that comes through me is from You. Use me to do Your will. Although I am persecuted by those that claim to know You I feel no pain. For You are with me and no harm shall come to me. No sadness shall prevent me from trying to serve You. Allow me to work for peace, fight for justice and add something positive to the world. Free me from the ignorance that allows others to call for war, spread hate and increase suffering. Open the minds and hearts of political and religious leaders so that they may spread Your commandment to love one another. Establish respect for all humans, especially those who are most oppressed.

For Eternity

Bring peace into my life, O Jesus Christ, and place me where I may best serve You. Reveal Your plan for me and allow me to accept the challenges that wait. Prevent me from losing site of the reason I am here – to prepare myself for Eternity with You. Allow me to rely on the many beautiful people that You have placed into my life as I struggle to reach my potential. Bless me with the courage to accept my limitations, the grace to deal with my faults and the mercy that You alone offer. Allow me to communicate Your greatness to all people, whoever they may be.

The Decision

O Jesus Christ, You have established within us the opportunity to know peace. Keep us open to our chance to serve those who have lost hope. Challenge us to see where our talents can bring forth-positive change. Give us the courage to go beyond what we consider familiar so that we may find solutions where we have failed to look. Lessen the division among those who have opposing views and increase our ability to recognize our common qualities. Allow those who struggle with tough decisions to be guided by Your holy wisdom and a clear vision of our reality. Be with us, O Jesus Christ and keep us aware of Your loving presence.

Consumption

Consume my heart with Your love, Jesus
Christ. Hasten my journey to openness,
honesty and truth. Bring peace into the lives
that I encounter and heal those who suffer.
Target with compassion those who have
isolated themselves through drugs, alcohol
and serious addiction. Deliver our world from
the course of bitterness, anger and injustice.
Bless us with peace and allow harmony to find
a place in our lives. May our days be filled
with the joy and sacred fulfillment that only
You offer.

The Calling

I offer my life to You, sweet Jesus Christ, for it is all that I have. Allow me to find my true calling in life and have the courage to accept it. As You created me to carry out this specific purpose, may I honor You in the manner in which I adopt it as my mission. Provide all people with the vision to see that we are here to serve You and that each of us is uniquely qualified to carry out one specific deed. May our diversity of service bring forth peace and healing throughout the world. No matter how small or how large the tasks that You have entrusted me, allow me to do it well and be pleasing to You.

All That I Am

Dear God, please allow me to use the blessings that You have bestowed upon me to see the goodness that surrounds me. May I use my ears to hear the words of peace and love that are spoken daily. May I use my eyes to see the work that others do to bring about justice and peace. May I use my mind to think positively of the world that You have lovingly created for me. May I use my hands to reach for those less fortunate. May I use my feet to travel on the path that You have laid before me. Finally, let me to use my heart to experience and share the love that only You allow. I ask this in Your name. Amen.

Examine

Dear Jesus Christ, we cherish the sacred blessing of Your friendship. Push us to examine our lives to see where we are failing to allow peace to take root. Free us from the sadness of prejudice, ignorance and racism. Challenge us to look beyond our differences so that we may see our common identity based in Your creation. Make each of us aware that we have been created in Your image and remind us that You reside within us. Increase self-esteem in all people and allow us to grow beyond the issues we dislike about ourselves, so that we may see beyond the weaknesses of others. Increase our commitment to peace and make Your presence known to those who live without You.

Chapter III

The
Peace
That Was
Meant
To Be

Escape

Dear Jesus Christ, You have blessed us richly. Bring peace to a society that has so much and yet yearns for that which they cannot name. Help us to save an entire generation determined to escape from reality through drugs and alcohol. Allow them to give life a chance, with a sober mind and the acceptance of Your love. Fill their void with the awareness of their sacred origin and the comfort of Your forgiveness. Present Yourself into their lives and let them see what was missing.

Hopelessness

O Jesus Christ, You have given us so much to enjoy. Bring peace to those who have a perceived absence of hope. Fill their life with meaning and lift the veil of depression that blinds them of the goodness surrounding them. Teach us to respect all people who deal with mental anxiety and allow new therapies to be discovered. Bless all people with the gift of hope and allow it to bring peace into our hearts, homes, country and world. Through You, all things are possible.

Pray for the Misguided

O loving God, allow me to do Your will. I pray for those that have turned to violence and live with hate-filled hearts. Provide them peace and understanding. Show them that You love them and that it will never be too late to come back to You. They have chosen to follow the misguided and have unfortunately been led away from You. Make them aware of Your unconditional love and forgiveness. Allow the true causes of injustice to be known. Protect us from evil and allow peace to spread throughout Your universe.

Transitions

Dear God, You are the stability that we rely upon. Bring peace to us as we make our way through life. Change is a very difficult and fearful aspect of maturing. Allow us the courage to accept new responsibilities and give us the grace to relinquish that which age no longer allows. Preserve our dignity and provide us with patience. Bless us with health and help as we make this transition. As Your children, we may not understand Your ways, but our faith in You will never die.

Gift of Christmas

May the gift of Christmas fill our hearts and
live within us throughout the year. May Jesus
Christ's compassion, be felt by all regardless
of one's faith. Allow us to give and receive
gifts, which truly celebrate the love that Jesus
Christ has for us. Bless our families and
friends with health, peace of mind and
prosperity. Renew our commitment to pray
for peace, work for justice, and to see You in
all people. We are eternally grateful for the
gift of life, the ability to love and that, which
sustains us – Hope.

A Child's Peace

You, God have blessed me with a father and
mother that have been the most wonderful
parts of my life. I have experienced security,
guidance and an unconditional love from
them, which has allowed me to experience a
life of peace. I am so proud that my life is the
fruit of their union. I pray for those that were
denied this relationship. Provide peace for
the children that are unwanted and reveal
Your power to those that are blessed with the
opportunity to have them.

Holiday Peace

Bless my family and friends O God as we begin to prepare for the approaching Holidays. Allow those who are stressed by strained relationships to find forgiveness and a sense of kindness for one another. Provide us with strong resolve to accept the differences that have placed a wedge between those we once loved. Renew respect within our family, as this is the primary element of peace. Have mercy on children of all ages who are faced with parents who live apart. Allow them to enjoy the season free from anxiety and parental selfishness. Finally, comfort those who will face this time alone. May they feel the love and peace of God from all those who know You.

Pain

You are the healer of the world, O Jesus Christ. Allow us to recognize the pain of insecurity that comes from an unstable world and not hide from it, ignore it, drug it or deny it. Teach us to respond to it, as we should with all pain. Let us work, change and sacrifice to bring forth true and lasting peace so that our pain can be healed. Give us the courage to seek remedies that do not rely on inflicting pain on others but bring healing comfort to all people in a world hemorrhaging with pain.

Justice

Come into our hearts, O God, and fill our days with peace. Teach us to live as examples of Your love and mercy. Make all people know that the cornerstone of peace is justice. Hunger, unemployment, disease and inadequate housing lead to desperation and despair. For those who are comfortable, may they know compassion. For those that are righteous, may they find humility, and to the uncaring, reveal Yourself in those they ignore. Challenge each of us to make a difference.

Peace to the Homeless

We sing Your praises throughout the land, O God. Bring peace to those men, women and children who find themselves without a home. Regardless of how these people ended up on the street, keep them safe and out of harm's way. Show Your mercy on those who are afflicted with mental disease or addiction. Allow loved ones who have lost touch with a homeless person to find peace and free them from endless worry. Keep our hearts open to the fact that each of these people are made in Your likeness and their misfortune should not allow us to dismiss them as less than ourselves.

Political Candidates

Provide guidance and wisdom dear God as I cast my vote for our political leaders. Let me not be swayed by self-serving agendas but allow me to support the individual who will work best to better our world. Give me an open mind and heart so that I may make myself available to different points of view. Lead me to those candidates that will govern with wisdom, work for justice and foster a peaceful community for us all. Finally, ease the pain for the candidates and families of those that fail in their attempts to be elected. Make them aware that their gifts and talents will be better utilized elsewhere in Your divine plan.

Long Goodbye

In You, O God, we find great comfort. Please bring peace to the victims of Alzheimer's disease. Although we are unable to communicate fully with them, allow our undying love and respect for them to be known. Bring peace and consolation to the families that deal with this sad condition. Allow them to remain hopeful and compassionate. Although it is like a long goodbye, keep us mindful that this suffering will be but for a moment when considering the eternal happiness that lies ahead.

Peace of Good Health

Bless us with the peace of good health, dear God. Allow our families to enjoy the comfort of our wellness. Please allow those that are burdened by the pain of sickness and disease, the opportunity to overcome these burdens and enjoy the gift of life. Keep us safe from all harm and let us accept the burdens that we do encounter as a way to bring us closer to You. We know that You alone are the Master and we lovingly submit to Your plan.

Peace in Nursing Homes

In You God, I find peace and comfort. Bestow Your peace upon those that are living in nursing homes and elderly care facilities. May they know the peace of compassion and allow their families to be free of the guilt that sometimes comes with these arrangements. Provide them with skilled care providers and allow their days to be filled with meaning. Allow them to grow in spirituality and may they not suffer from loneliness. If and when it is necessary for me to face life in a nursing home, allow me to accept it with grace, ease the burden on my family and fill my days with Your peace.

Peace at Work

Loving and ever-living God, You are the provider of all that we need. Bless those who are starting a new workweek. May they know peace at work, as well as at home. Provide a safe and enjoyable environment for them and may their labors bring them rich reward. Bless all those who seek employment with new opportunities and protect them from self-doubt. You have blessed each of us with many gifts. Allow us to share them in ways that honor You. For in You, we find our peace.

Peace after the Storm

We sing Your praises God throughout the land. Bring peace to all those who have been affected by natural disasters. So many lives are changed in mere moments from storms, earthquakes and tornadoes. Many will never recover from this devastation and will experience difficult tests of faith. You have told us that we shall not know the day or the moment that our life on earth will end. We ask that all those who have lost their lives recently, be taken into Your kingdom and their loved ones be blessed with the peace of knowing that You are always with them. Allow communities to rebuild their homes, strengthen their faith in You and grow in the love of their neighbor.

Peace to the Lonely

Bring peace to the lonely, O God for their
burden is heavy. Allow them to recognize the
beauty they possess as an individual. Free
them from despair and hopelessness. Teach
them to look outward so that they may add
their talents to a society that may seem
uncaring. Peace needs to start from within so
that it can be spread throughout Your family.
We pray for those that are unable to see
through the dark shadows of depression.
May Your peace offer them rest and
happiness.

Peace to Teens

In You, O God, I have found peace. Each of us is blessed with the many gifts that You have generously bestowed upon us. In Your mercy, provide a peaceful transition to all those who are living out their teenage years. This time is filled with new opportunities and many choices. Few are easy to make and often the lines are blurred between adult choices and those that should be made by a child. Allow them the freedom to exercise their newfound maturity but provide parental guidance when it is needed. Do not allow parents to forget their responsibilities and bless them with patience. Keep all of them safe and guide them to follow the path that leads to You. Give each family that is dealing with this situation the peace to remain a loving and nurturing part of Your creation.

Peace in Marriage

We pray for those that are about to be married. May their lives be filled with peace. Bring joy to the families of those involved and may they be supportive and accepting of the newly formed union. Provide patience to each individual as they adjust to a new life of sharing, sacrificing and newness. Finally, bless all relationships that are based in Your love. To love is a remarkable gift from You that we cherish.

Pray for the Media

Holy and Everlasting God, my love for You brings great comfort to me. Bless those that work in the media. Keep them safe from undue influence and allow them to do their job in a way that honors You with the Truth. Keep them safe when they are in harms way. Do not permit them from stressing their own agenda. Give them and their superiors the wisdom to report the facts regardless of who is involved. Perhaps the knowledge that they bring to us will allow justice to prevail and make way for a world filled with peace.

Prison

In You, O Jesus Christ, we are set free. Bring peace to all men and women who face life in prison. May they find self-worth, self-forgiveness and hope. Ease their loneliness and raise their self-esteem. Bring peace to the victims of their crimes and allow them to be able to forgive in order to set themselves free of their pain. Have mercy on the families of criminals and allow them to live free of guilt and shame. Teach all of us to work for the causes of justice, equality and fairness. Touch my heart so that I may be able to forgive.

Service Workers

O God, You have placed wonderful people in our lives. Bring peace to those individuals who work to make life better. Watch over utility workers as they strive to restore electricity, remove snow, fight fires and come to our aid. Protect police officers as they protect us. Allow medical professionals to feel the comfort that they bring to the sick and their families. Bless religious leaders with reward for the blessings that they bring into our lives. Guide and watch over all of these people as they serve their fellowman.

Retirement Prayer

Thank You, O God, for allowing me to reach
this point in my life. Today I retired from my
job and opened the door to the next part of
my life. Guide me through this tough transition
and provide me with purpose, good health
and peace of mind. Allow me to enjoy the
fruits of my many years of work. Bless my
family with financial peace and allow us to
grow closer as we enjoy the opportunity to be
with one another. May I use this time to enjoy
Your creation, bring happiness to those
around me and relax in the knowledge of Your
love. As Your child may I be poor in
misfortune, rich in blessings, slow to make
enemies, quick to make friends. But rich or
poor, quick or slow, may I know nothing but
peace from this day forward.

Sobriety

O Loving God, You are the freedom that we seek. Free us from the pains of addiction and restore our health. End the trafficking of drugs and violence that feed our cravings. Fill the emptiness that we have with Your peace. Save our families from the temptations of drug-induced escape. Show us the rewards of sobriety and give us the strength to persevere. Lead all of Your children to live lives with meaning and to serve those who are in need.

Troubled Hearts

Eternal God, You bless us with Your unending gift of love. Provide peace to those who are contemplating suicide. Allow the darkness to pass from their thoughts and provide them with hope. Make them aware of the love that You and others have for them. Intercede on behalf of those who are unaware of the pain that the person is experiencing. Protect that person from bringing harm to themselves and show them that the troubles of this world are temporary. Give them strength to accept what they cannot change, hope to expect improvements and self-forgiveness so that they may know peace.

Those that Suffer

Hold us in Your kind embrace, dear God, and protect us from all harm. Show Your infinite mercy upon those that are suffering from disease, especially AIDS. Entire countries are threatened by this terrible epidemic that adds to the suffering of many generations. Show Your compassion to those unable to acquire medical treatment and allow the distribution of medicine to flow freely. Remove the social and political stigma from AIDS and allow a cure to be found. Bring peace to all families that have suffered this agony. In You, all things are possible.

Waiting

Hold me, O God, and keep me close to You.
Bring peace of mind to those people who are
living in agony as they await the results of
medical tests. Draw them close and let them
know that You are waiting with them. Comfort
them with the peace that only You can give.
Bless all people who face a risk to their
health. It is not only the suffering that they
fear but how their lives might change. Life is
so precious and any threat to it fills us with
despair. We pray for a positive report but if it
is not to be, then give us the strength to
accept a negative prognosis and the will to go
on living.

Working Poor

All knowing and ever-loving God, we sing Your praises throughout the land. Bring peace to the working poor. Comfort those who live from paycheck to paycheck. Remove the stress that comes from the constant worry of struggling to survive. Allow them to find a new means of income and keep their faith strong. Allow us to offer a helping hand to those who are too proud to ask. Ease our desire for material possessions and keep us on the path that leads to You.

Unending Circle

O Jesus Christ, You satisfy our every need. Bring peace to our lives and allow us to reclaim our divine destiny. Give us the strength to turn from excessive eating, drinking and drug abuse that ultimately increases our distance from You. Let us find comfort in the one and true nourishment – Your love. Allow those that feel helpless against the addictions that rule their lives to find an escape from their misery. Break the vicious circle that feeds our addictions and adds to our woes. Increase our self-esteem by a renewed awareness that we are Your children.

God is the Path and Destination

Most holy God, You are both the path and destination that I seek. In You I am able to see clearly the splendor of Your universe and the hope for Eternity. Keep me close to You and do not allow me to stray from the path that You have laid before me. Watch over my family and protect them from all evils that may harm them. Keep safe the innocent and let them know Your love. Have mercy on those that are afflicted with physical or mental problems and allow them to know true peace.

Memorial

You are the path, the sacred road that leads
to true life, dear Jesus Christ. Prevent us
from traveling farther on the violent road that
we have chosen and give us new direction for
the way in which we deal with our problems.
With peace as our destination, guide us to
bring forth justice. Keep us aware of the
travesty of war and the long lasting affects it
has for generations. Teach us to forgive,
trust and work together to bring forth a true
and everlasting peace. Allow us to remember
those who have offered their lives in the
hopes that others will have a better and more
rewarding future. Grant them peace.

The Birth

Prepare our hearts, O Jesus Christ, for the peaceful changes that are about to be born. Come into our lives today, just as Innocence was made flesh so long ago. May the time not be so distant when, once again, the world shall awaken to a new beginning. A new awakening that will encompass the earth and man shall know You and turn quickly from the ways of evil. All pain and misery shall be forgotten and goodness shall triumph from that day forward. No longer shall we hunger for nourishment and love, but we shall spend every moment feeding upon Your compassion. Come, O Jesus Christ, for Your children are ready.

Peace in our Schools

Restore peace to our schools, O God and
return them to an atmosphere of learning.
Bring about respect for all teachers from
students and parents. Keep us safe from
fellow students who are misguided and cry
out for attention through violence. Allow what
we learn to be used to better our lives, help
our community and solve some of the
problems that exist in the world. Guide us
through education to live as children of Your
divine plan.

Peace in Friendship

Heal my broken heart, O God and show
mercy on those that I have hurt. You blessed
me with the wonderful gift of a best friend and
I have allowed pride, selfishness and anger to
harm the relationship. It was such a small thing
that caused this problem but I refused to
forgive and now I am filled with loneliness and
despair. Bless all forms of friendship and
remind us of their value. If it is Your will, then
allow me to restore my relationship so that I
may once again enjoy the peace found
through friendship.

Songs Never Sung

In You God, I am whole. Bless with peace those who are troubled by depression, guilt and acute anxiety. Allow them to live fully and share the gifts that You have bestowed upon them. Their lives are like songs never sung. Free them from the self-imprisonment they experience. Have mercy on the families that deal with this struggle and grant them Your peace.

Prayer for Relationships

Bring peace, O God, to those who find themselves in broken relationships. Bring forth forgiveness to those who are unable to offer it. Protect the children whose parents are separated or divorced. Let them know security. Bless the troubled with wisdom and allow them to keep themselves available to reconciliation. Show us that compromise, selflessness, and patience can heal many broken hearts. Bless our families and friends with Your peace.

Growing Old

God, comfort me as I grow old. Provide me with a peaceful life so that I may enjoy Your abundant gifts. Allow me to accept the mental and physical changes that go along with ageing. Watch over my family and friends as they too mature and face new challenges with health and mobility. Do not permit pride to interfere with allowing others to do for me what I have done for them. I accept the slowing of my mind and body as it allows more time to communicate my love and devotion to You. Guide me through this part of my life so that I will be most ready to join You in Eternity.

Rejoice

Rejoice in the wonders of Jesus Christ. Rejoice that we have received the gift of Jesus Christ's love. Find comfort in the blessings of hope and compassion. Allow the spirit of Christmas to transform our lives and exemplify Jesus Christ's glory. Bring each of us to a new awareness of the sanctity of peace. The dream that Jesus Christ has for the world is so much larger than what we could ever imagine. Restore our child-like hearts so that we may realize our true potential. Free us from that which prevents us from accepting the true gift of Christmas – Peace.

Great and Small

O Jesus Christ, Your splendor is revealed in all creatures, great and small. Thank You for the comfort, joy and peace that members of the animal kingdom bring into our lives. Have mercy on those innocent beings that are abused or neglected by their keepers. Teach us to learn from the example of pets that display total loyalty, unconditional love and pure devotion. Allow our hearts to be as forgiving as those seen in our animal friends. Bring peace to our hearts when we must deal with the death of a beloved pet. Find a special place for them and bless them with Your compassion.

Those that Struggle

Loving God, we know that You will never give us more than we can handle. Show mercy on those people that are starting to have doubts. Bless them with peace and bring hope into their lives. Give them strength to face each challenge and strengthen their faith. Let them know that they are not alone and that You will bring them comfort. Teach us all to seize opportunities that could lessen the burden on our fellowman. Lift up our spirits and bless our lives with peace.

Corner Stones

Fill us with Your sacred power to see the basic
goodness in all creation, O Jesus Christ.
Enable us to discover the elements of
forgiveness, hospitality and generosity. Bring
peace to our hearts and allow it to flow forth
throughout the Universe. Have mercy on
those who face a lifetime of suffering from
war, chaos and disenchantment. Reveal
Yourself from within each of us and allow
others to know the joy that You offer. May
peace become the cornerstone of our
generation and the foundation for building a
glorious future.

Childhood

Holy and loving, Jesus Christ, You have
blessed us with abundant treasures. Fill our
children with the peace of innocence. Allow
them to grow and mature in the comfort of
healthy parents, loving homes and with the
gift of Your Presence. Teach them to believe
in themselves, trust in others and to know that
with You all things are possible. Protect them
from all harms and give them the opportunity
to live in a world on the brink of peace.
Challenge all of us to respect the importance
of childhood and renew the spirit of youth
within each of us.

Alone

In You, O God, we find great comfort. Bring peace to those who are lonely. Place someone in their lives that will bring joy and security. Help those looking for a new relationship to find someone who can enrich their life. Teach us to seek out those who may feel abandoned and provide company to those who are alone. May the peace of Your love touch all of our hearts and stay with us all the days of our lives.

Addiction

In You Jesus Christ, we find our strength. Renew peace and security within our neighborhoods. Alleviate the pains of drug and alcohol addiction that have harmed our relationships with those around us and with You. To those involved in the trafficking of drugs, lessen the seduction of quick money and reveal the sadness that the industry promotes. Give us the courage to face our addictions, the ability to recover from them and the rewards that sobriety offers.

Abuse Victim

In You, I find all of my comfort. Bring peace,
reconciliation and purpose to the lives of
those who have been traumatized by abuse
and betrayal. Guide them to move forward
with their lives so that the abuser fails in their
attempt to control. Prevent them from giving
up on life because of past wrongs and
provide them with health of mind and body.
Teach us to have empathy and understanding
for what the innocent victim feels and protect
all of Your children from individuals who have
lost their way. Justice is Yours, O God.

Respect Life

Most holy and ever-living God, in You we find
our peace. Renew respect for all life,
regardless of its nature. Allow us to accept
the mystery of creation and Your divine plan.
Prevent those who feel inconvenienced by
life's challenges from committing acts that
distinguish life. As our God, You have chosen
the moment of our birth and the moment of
our death. Bless us with the courage to honor
Your will and open the hearts of those who
are about to choose their own destiny.

Dealing with Cancer
(for Joanie)

O God, Your power and mercy fill us with hope. Bring peace and healing to my loved one as they begin their battle with cancer. Lessen the pain and suffering that we must endure. Fill our hearts with trust as we place our concerns in Your hands. Teach us to see the goodness that comes from life's challenges and strengthen our faith in the power of prayer. Remain close to the family as they face the uncertainty that cancer brings. Do not allow them to live in fear and keep them ever aware of the tremendous love and support that surrounds them. Bless those who will provide treatment with the talent that shall bring forth the miracle of healing that comes from You. Have mercy on all people who deal with cancer and protect them from all harm. We ask for our loved one's full and speedy recovery as we praise Your marvelous name.

Chapter IV

With
God
As
Our
Father

Smile

Smile and be happy, for we are the blessed children of Jesus Christ. Keep us aware that in You all things are possible. Transform our lives so that others may come to know the depth of Your love. Manifest in us the gift of peace that comes through You. Touch the hearts of those who live in darkness and brighten their lives with hope. Resolve the issues that hold the world down and lift up our spirit so that others may believe. Thank You for giving us the gift of faith, the courage to hope and the blessing of heart-felt peace.

Peace to You

Loving God, You have provided us with abundant joy. Bless with peace, each person that says this prayer. You know our every need and desire. Do what is best for us and allow peace to fill our hearts. Some of us need financial peace, while others seek peace within their family. We all pray for peace to spread throughout the world and know that in You, all thinks are possible. Thank You for the special blessings that You have shared with us.

Miracle of Life

That which You have created, O God, is the evidence of Your majesty. Bless those who have doubt in You with the gift of peace. May they see Your hand in all they encounter. Forgive those of us who have been given the gift of faith, as we still look for miraculous signs of Your presence. We should be able to watch the smallest seed transform itself into a mighty tree and know that You are there. Teach us to accept the wonder that You have bestowed upon us.

Be at Peace

In You, God, we find our peace. Allow us to become still and rest in Your loving presence. Find a quiet place for us to escape the demands that are placed upon us. Clear our minds of the static that prevents our communion with You. Teach us to retreat from a life filled with temptations, distractions and anarchy. Guide us to find simplicity. Lift the burden of stress and renew our hearts so that we may become people of peace.

Sanctuary

You see directly into our souls, O Jesus
Christ. Bless our places of worship with Your
sacred protection. Do not allow them to be
used for anything less than pure and reverent
adoration of You. Fill these establishments
with Your peace and allow them to be centers
that openly welcome all who want to become
closer to You. Increase our respect for all
faiths and allow understanding to end our
ability to cause pain to those we fear. May all
those who seek refuge be blessed with Your
compassion and for all those who seek
forgiveness be overcome by Your mercy.

Anchor and Compass

You provide us with the strength to endure all hardship, O Jesus Christ. Bring peace to those who suffer from the storms of nature, the sadness of loneliness and the heartaches of war. Place Your sacred protection around those who are most vulnerable to danger and allow Your presence to be felt when it is most needed. Guide us to find shelter from that which enables pain and hardship to endure. Allow our pain to be the catalyst for positive change and a new resolve to live in Your peace. Challenge us to see beyond the current storm so that we may envision the great reward that You have designed for us. Be our anchor and our compass, as we stay grounded in our journey to You.

Ashes

O Jesus Christ, You have orchestrated both
life and death. Allow us to live in peace and
harmony while we work to serve You.
Challenge us to accept our limitations and
give us the strength to carry out Your will.
Keep us ever mindful of our chief concern –
to serve You. Allow us to love You more each
day, for this is where pleasure presides.
Keep us on the path that leads to Your
Eternal reward and help us to find positive
solutions to life's most demanding hardships.
Welcome each of us into Your Home when
You are most ready to receive us and grant
that others may know the peace of Your love.

Divine Creator

Most holy and ever-living God, I come before You in heartfelt appreciation for all that You have bestowed upon me. I marvel at Your wonderful creation and I am humbled to think that a power so great and wondrous as You created me, unique from every other person before me and after me, to fit into Your divine creation. I am filled with peace, knowing that You loved me enough to give me life. You have shown Your trust in me through the responsibilities that have been laid before me. You have shown Your mercy by the forgiveness that You alone can offer and You have provided me with a deep faith which has become the foundation of peace in my life. Allow my actions to honor You.

Ecstasy

O Jesus Christ, You are the Light that shines throughout the world. Change our despair into hope. Fill every corner of the universe with Your holy love and allow peace to manifest where it has been abandoned. Save us from our commitment to solve our problems without Your guidance. Allow the spirit of forgiveness, charity and humility to fill our lives and direct us to surrender ourselves to Your power. Sustain us with Your mercy, fill us with Your grace and grant us the ecstasy that comes in knowing You.

Enlightenment

In You, O God, everything is possible.
Enlighten those who are unable to accept
Your mercy. Restore sight to those blinded by
hate. Feed the souls of those starved by Your
absence. Awaken the spirit of sleeping hearts
and shed light upon the paths of darkness.
Allow the goodness of humanity to shine so
brightly that all evil is overshadowed. Permit
us to serve You by sharing the gift of peace.
May no one miss the rewards of Your love.

Evening Prayer for Peace

We praise You God and thank You for this
day. May the manner in which we have spent
today honor You. Please grant us peace and
rest so that we may reflect upon the blessings
that You have bestowed upon us. Let us
awake to a world renewed in Your love and
respect for our fellow man. Please allow us to
see the true universe that You have created,
free of war, hate and fear. Let us keep in mind
that we are here for such a brief time and that
each moment is to be enjoyed and lived
celebrating Your love for us. Amen.

Faith

My faith in You, Dear God, brings me endless peace. Touch the hearts of those that have lost their faith. Perhaps they felt rejected, saw hypocrisy or simply lost their way. Have mercy on them and place an opportunity in their lives that will cause them to awaken. Bring peace to all parents whose children have abandoned their spiritual family. May they know Your unconditional and all-forgiving love. It is together in faith that we are one.

Forgiveness

Most Holy and everlasting God, we are
blessed to be Your children. Lead us to the
path of forgiveness, so that we may enjoy
peace in our hearts. You were able to forgive
us so completely that all remembrance of our
most grave sin has been forgotten.
Forgiveness offers us the opportunity to
open ourselves more completely to You. It
frees us from the weight of bitterness, hatred
and self-pity. Lighten our hearts, so that we
may become better people, able to spread
the message of love and peace that You have
provided. In You alone, we find our peace.

Gift of Faith

Thank You, O God, for providing me with a
strong faith in You and all of Your children.
Bring peace to those who are trying to believe
in You and have been unable to accept Your
love. Provide them with patience and reveal
Yourself to them. The pain of not knowing
You is surely unbearable. Use the faithful to
provide witness to those who are seeking.
Peace is my gift from You. Allow me to share
this precious gift.

Glory to God

O most holy God, I honor and love You with all of my being. I thank You for the gifts that I have received. You have blessed me with the gift of unconditional love from my family and friends. You have shown me never ending forgiveness in spite of my failures. You have shown me true Peace in the darkest of times and every opportunity has been laid before me. Although I am weak, give me the courage to live my life as an example of Your will. I pray that I may spread the message of peace so that I can concentrate on the splendor of Your Universe. In You alone, I find peace.

God's Compassion

All powerful and ever-living God, we praise Your glory and miraculous works. We ask that You bless us with health, prosperity and peace. Please allow us to live in a way that is pleasing to You. Allow us to make time for You so that we may simply enjoy Your presence. Strengthen our faith in You and open the hearts of the non-believers that they may experience the ecstasy of Your love. Show us Your compassion when we offend You and make us humble when we start to venture from the divine path that You have offered us. Allow me to live as an example of Your love.

God's Peace

In God, I have found peace. You comfort me in all aspects of my life. How do I find room for doubt? As always, You guide me in the right direction. You alone know my every need. The life that You have provided for me is pure joy. I am so grateful for all that You have provided. Please allow me to share Your gift of peace.

Gratitude

Most holy God, You have given so much and our limitations as humans prohibit us from being able to express our gratitude in the manner in which we would like. As innocent children, we rely upon You for all nourishment, protection, guidance and care. Although the child is unable to express appreciation, the parent is richly satisfied. Allow us to reveal hearts filled with unspeakable gratitude. We have peace in knowing that You are there.

Heal

O Divine Comforter, bless us with Your sacred presence. Bring healing to those who thirst for Your salvation. Bestow upon us the miracle of Your love, the gift of Your friendship and the joy of Your peace. Heal those who suffer from spiritual blindness, physical challenge or mental anxiety. Bless those who suffer from addiction, abuse or an absence of knowing Your forgiveness. Console those who seek understanding, guidance and self-worth.

Hear the prayer of those who are desperately seeking escape from constant pain, disease, misunderstanding or the agony of loss. Lift us from despair, hopelessness and depression. Touch the hearts of those who suffer from broken relationships, families in crisis and loneliness. Grant that we may see You in our daily lives, and grow to rely upon

Your unending ability to heal and to nurture. Grant that we may see You in all people regardless of appearance, circumstance or plight.

O God, heal our world. Free us from hate, injustice and war. Diminish the evil power of religious intolerance, political strife and racism and allow respect to penetrate our minds and actions. Teach us to live as You created us in Your own image.

Increase our capacity to love You and those around us more each day. Keep us ever aware of Your ability to heal and accept our never ending love and devotion to You. Amen

Guide Me Lord

God, Your love for me is immeasurable and I
cherish the intimacy that I share with You.
Deliver me from the oppression that keeps me
from knowing Your peace. Free me from the
prison of depression, illness and
hopelessness. Allow me to respect each day
as if it were the only one remaining. You have
given many gifts and I am grateful. From this
day forward let me remember that You are the
guide and I am the follower.

Honor

You fill us with Your peace, O Jesus Christ.
Blanket our lives with the blessings that You
offer. Bring comfort to those who suffer
from loneliness, isolation and depression.
Allow us to become aware of our ability to
honor You more often. Keep us mindful of
the rich gifts that we have been given, bring
people closer to You, and grant us the joy of
Your constant presence.

Inner Voice

You are my one and only guide, O Jesus
Christ. Allow me to listen to the small inner
voice hidden deep within my heart that tells
me to honor Your commands. Stop me from
climbing aboard the bandwagon and justifying
war. Reveal to us a sound and merciful
manner in which to protect ourselves while
respecting the lives of the innocent. Show me
where I have erred in allowing injustice to exist
for my own selfish purposes and give me the
courage to correct my wrongs. It is never too
late with You, Jesus Christ.

Isolation

O Jesus Christ, You see all things in a true
and perfect light. Bring peace to those who
search for answers to life's most mysterious
questions. Teach us to trust in Your wisdom
and to accept the reality that Your ways are
different from our ways. Allow each of us to
grow through our hardships and challenges.
Make Your presence felt by those who are
tempted to turn away from You. Do not allow
grief or anger to manifest itself into isolation
from Your love. Restore our innocence and
forgive us for the times that we have
abandoned You. Allow us to serve those who
are in need and permit them to see You from
within us.

Selflessness

All glory and honor to You, O God. You have
blessed our lives richly and Your love is
everlasting. Bless the lives of those who live
out of the spotlight. Allow them to know
peace. These are the individuals who spread
Your message of love without seeking notice
or self-reward. May they shine as an example
to all who try to elevate themselves through
their public deeds. Teach us all to live lives
that honor You while building communities
that celebrate all that You have created. Not
from me God, but You through me.

Show Us Peace

In You, with You and For You we live. As Your children we have been created in Your image. Allow us to see the beauty in all of our brothers and sisters so that we may live as the family that You have planned. Show us peace in our hearts, our homes and throughout Your world. We pray that we may know the true peace that comes from You.

Unanswered Prayers

You, O God, are kind and merciful. You know
our every need. Bring peace to those who
have unanswered prayers. May they come to
realize that Your divine plan will bring them
greater rewards than what they seek. Expose
the world to the gift of prayer. Open the lines
of communication between Yourself and
those that do not know how to pray. Allow
this bridge to provide the path to peace-filled
hearts and lives rich in spirit.

Simply God

O God, Your simplicity magnifies Your greatness. Bring peace to those who strive to condemn others in Your name. Touch their hearts and make them aware that You have things under control. Was it not You who created each of us in Your image? Was it not You who instructed us to love one another? Please teach us to accept this simple command. Allow those who feel the need to judge, to forgive themselves and open their hearts to Your mercy and compassion.

Accepted Blessings

Happy are we who have been blessed with Your constant presence. Bless us with a renewed belief in Your power to blanket the earth with peace. Challenge us to accept the blessings that you have prepared for us and bestow upon us the gift of serving You. Make each day a testimony of our love for You and allow others to find the source of Your compassion. Keep us faithful to Your command to love one another and guide us to find new answers to ancient conflicts. Free us from the agony of our past mistakes and allow us to live fully aware of the glory of Your creation.

Blessed by the Light

You are the Light of the Universe, O God and You are the brightness that we adore. Bring peace to those who live in the darkness. Some people have chosen to deny You but many, many people have not been blessed with knowing You. Teach parents to educate their children of Your marvelous works. Open every nation that oppresses its people and forbids them from spreading Your love. Allow us to be the spark that spreads light throughout the world where darkness grows. Allow us to shine as Children of God.

Divine Making

You breathe life into our world, O Jesus Christ. Fill us with Your compassion and allow us to know the unconditional love that You offer. Teach us to accept Your sacred gifts free from the conditions that man has placed upon them. Give us the courage to live the unique life that You have created for us and allow us to be an example for those who are unable to believe in their own divine making. Grant us the peace that only comes from You and deliver us from the forces that seek to divide us from You. Accept our love.

Thank You God

We thank You, Dear God, for granting us life
and for the peace that we have in knowing
You. You have bestowed great things upon all
of Your people and we appreciate the
individuals that You have placed in our lives.
We appreciate the spiritual awakening that
the world is experiencing. Finally, we are
overcome with gratitude for the gift of life and
the opportunity to serve You.

Awareness

O Jesus Christ, we long for the day that we see Your face. Bless us with the full awareness of Your constant presence. Like the air that we breathe, keep us mindful that You are beside us always. Allow our actions and words to reflect our recognition of Your closeness. May the keen sense of Your presence bring all of us to treat one another with love and respect. Perhaps then shall we be ready to accept Your gift of peace.

Absence of Faith

The rewards of my life, O Jesus Christ, are measured by the joy that Your love brings to me. Open the hearts of the non-believer, so that they may find meaning, comfort and peace. Allow them to feel the security that comes from unwavering faith in Your promises. Forgive those who have foolishly denied Your existence. Fill their emptiness with the courage to accept that even they are worthy of Your love and that Your mercy is without end. Renew our commitment to see You in all people.

Chapter V

Brothers
All
Are
We

Left Behind

You are our comfort, O Jesus. Watch over the children that have been left behind, as their parents are deployed to military service. Do not allow them to suffer from anxiety, depression and loneliness. May they live in the security of good and proper guardians during this trying time. Bring their parents safely home and end the need for their service as soon as possible. Allow us to be deeply aware of these children, regardless of the flag their mom or dad wears. Free us from the misery of war and allow peace to take hold.

Reveal Yourself

We need peace, O God, and through You we shall find it. Break down the fences that divide us from our enemies. Wash away our blindness and allow us to see You in faces of all skin colors. Let us hear Your word regardless of the tongue that it is spoken in. Allow us to feel Your warmth from those that we fear. Silence our call for war so that we may hear Your voice in every human that will suffer from aggression. Allow those who advocate terror to see us as humans, faithful to Your commandment of love and merciful to our enemies. When we are able to see You in those that we fear, then we shall have peace.

Rejects

O Jesus Christ, Your compassion and
unconditional love are constantly with us.
Bring peace to those who suffer from
constant loneliness. Fill our lives with
fellowship and meaning. Eliminate the
insecurity that prevents us from accepting
ourselves and limits our ability to welcome
people into our lives. Embrace those who are
seen as the rejects of society and reveal Your
sacred brilliance of creating each person
uniquely qualified to fulfill their purpose.
Remain close to those who live in doubt and
increase our faith in all that You offer.

Numbers

You have blessed us all with so many unique and wonderful gifts, O God. Prevent us from accepting the grim news of murder and terrorism as just more statistics. We hear each day of how a certain number of people died or the number of those injured in war and terrorist attacks. Keep us aware that each number represents a once living person. A person that had dreams, gifts to share and people who loved them. Do not allow us to accept the loss that each statistic represents.

Perfection

O Jesus Christ, You are perfection. Bring peace into our lives and allow us to recognize the talent and goodness that is embodied in our brothers and sisters. Make us aware of the heroes that walk with us in our everyday lives. How is it that we do not know the names of the brave astronauts that escape the gravity of earth until we are faced with tragedy or the miracles performed through doctors and nurses until mistakes are made? Also, how does the endless work of religious leaders and lay people go uncelebrated until scandal and weakness is displayed by the few? Perhaps it is like You, dear Jesus Christ. When all is perfect we sometimes fail to recognize Your presence. Teach us to see You in all Your children, including those who most reflect Your image.

Brother's Keeper

We are Your children, dear Jesus Christ, made in Your image and likeness. Allow me to see You in my brothers and sisters, regardless of where they have allowed themselves to go. Free them from the darkness of addiction and create an intervention that will restore their vision. Let them believe in themselves. They live in an absence of hope. Open their mind and heart to know that their divine creation demands nothing less than rising to capture their fullest potential. Teach them to look outward, to see the needs of others and to reclaim their life, which was created and nurtured by You. Do not allow me to enable their destruction, but keep me ever aware that I am my brother's keeper. In You Jesus Christ, all things are possible. Bring peace to all families faced with the agony of addiction.

Color Blind

All powerful and ever-living God, You have created each of us in Your likeness. Bring peace to those who are unable to get beyond racial boundaries. Open their hearts and minds and free them from this backwardness. It is our duty to work and live with all people as You have placed them in our lives. Teach us to see the unique individuals that You have created and put an end to racial oppression. Allow our leaders to confront their prejudices and govern with equality and respect for all people.

Daily Peace

Ever-loving God, teach me to love those who
are difficult to like. Teach me to care for
those who do not care for me. Give me
courage to face that which I fear. Allow me to
find goodness in the worst of people. Free me
from the prison of ignorance and prejudice.
Unlock the chains of guilt and regret. Allow
me to convey the truth to those who live in
falsehood. Let me comfort those who deny
You. May I live until I die, may I love You more
each day and may lasting peace come upon
every person that You place into my life.

Lessen the Load

We are blessed to live in Your presence, Jesus Christ. Bring peace to families where turmoil has taken root. Eliminate worries of financial pressures, insecurity and boredom. Renew commitments that have become lost in the day-to-day occurrences that frequent our lives. Bring a new sense of awareness to those we encounter and allow us to open our hearts to those who long for acceptance. End our day with the reward of having lessened the load of someone in need. Remain close to us in all that we attempt and guide us to the rewards that You offer.

Joys of Peace

Bring peace into our lives, O Jesus Christ.
Allow us to master Your commandment to love
one another before all else. Extinguish our
desire to stand in judgment, for You alone are
able to see into the hearts of Your children.
Teach us to respect all people of faith and
allow us to work toward common goods.
Strengthen our resolve to work for justice so
that we may rediscover the joys of peace.

One in You

In You, God, we shall find our peace. Comfort those who find themselves spending the holidays away from those they love. Allow them to be close in heart and in spirit. Provide us with opportunities to be together in the near future and keep us safe from all harm. We especially pray for those in the military who have been called to foreign lands by their leaders. Bless them with a special peace that only You can provide. Have mercy on their families and ease their anxiety. Allow us to be as one as we celebrate Your greatness.

Chapter VI

In
Perfect
Harmony

The Presence

Your peace fills our lives with joy, O Jesus
Christ. Bless this season with the gifts of
love, simplicity and spiritual harmony. Grant
healing where suffering exists and bring
compassion into the lives that most need Your
help. Give us the courage to amend our lives
so that we may embrace all that You have
planned for us. Allow peace to be known by
all people and keep us constantly aware of
Your sacred presence.

Prayer for Newborns

O mighty and ever-living God, we proclaim Your goodness throughout the world. Your creation is filled with so many unique pieces and together they proclaim Your glory. We ask that You bless every newborn person with the gift of peace. May they be allowed to grow up in a world filled with love and free from violence, injustice and war. Provide them with a loving family so that they may be able to love in a healthy manner. Give them security so that they will not be influenced by fear. Show them the ways of justice so that they may bring about peace and give them the gift of faith so that they may live in Your warm compassion.

We Pray

We pray for the lonely, may they know the love that only You provide. We pray for the broken spirit of the poor, may they know the hope that You offer. We pray for the sick, may they feel Your healing touch. We pray for the weak, may they experience justice, which brings Your ultimate gift which is peace. Amen

Mercy

O Merciful Jesus Christ, we find our peace in You. Teach us to be able to forgive those who have caused us pain. The simple act of forgiveness is how we may best portray Your love for us and is the single step that we can take which leads to the healing of the world. Free us from the bonds of revenge, resentment, bitterness and hatred. Allow us to live with love-filled hearts, ever aware of Your immediate presence.

Live Your Life

O Loving God, You have blessed each one of
us with a splendid and remarkable gift of life.
Bring peace to those who feel they must live
their life for someone else. Give them the
courage to live the life You have created and
with which You have entrusted them. Show us
that each unique life is like a single brush
stroke and together Your wondrous
masterpiece is revealed. Allow us to accept
those people who are different from us and
see Your marvelous works in them.

Homage

To You, sweet Jesus Christ, we pay homage.
Allow us to find inner peace and protect us
from all harm. Free us from the misery of
depression, illness and worry. Teach us to
live in the presence of the life, which You have
Blessed us. Grant that we may become more
aware of the needs of others and give us the
courage to make amends where we have done
wrong. Keep us centered on Your law – to
love one another. Strengthen our resolve to
make the most of our lives while being
committed to doing that, which pleases You.

Gather Us In

Gather us in, O God. We are looking in a thousand different places for answers that elude us. You have given us the solution that will bring about peace and yet we look elsewhere. Gather us in dear God. Remind us again of how to live in a peaceful and peace-filled world. Gather us in almighty God. Show us that Your simple message is the key to the universal quest for peace. Gather us in Eternal God. Open our minds and our hearts so that we may accept Your most powerful commandment – Love one another. Gather us in O God.

Family in Turmoil

Dear God, have mercy on me, and my family. We no longer live as a family should. We have been affected by drug and alcohol abuse and we no longer show respect to each other. Although we feel unworthy of Your love, bless us with Your peace. Try to forgive us as we make our way back to You. We have allowed the seduction of addiction to pull us away from You and Your promise of Eternity. Provide us with some hope that the road we travel will not lead to death. We know that our actions are wrong and offend You, but we are weak and need Your grace to overcome this challenge in our lives. Please protect my family and allow them to stay together. I pray for peace.

Open Our Minds

Open our minds and our hearts dear God,
that we may hear You. May Your voice calm all
people and put us on the path to
reconciliation, justice and peace. Provide
guidance for those who feel hopeless. Keep
them from accepting the ways of evil and give
them courage so that they may work for
peace. Provide food for the hungry, drink for
those that thirst and hope for those that do
not know You. You have created each of us in
Your image. Allow us to reflect the peace that
You alone offer.

Burn

We are Your humble servants, O Jesus Christ.
Place us where we are most able to do Your
work. Allow us to be the instruments of Your
peace and push us to follow the paths that
You lay before us. Challenge us to overcome
our apprehension as we look at the tragedy
we have created. Bless all people with the
vision to see the brevity of our life and the
remarkable opportunity to make this a better
world. Burn our hearts with Your love, our
minds with the determination to succeed and
our souls with the joy of Your presence.

Children of God

O God, You have surrounded us with a world filled with remarkable people. Bring peace and special blessings to all those who add goodness and kindness to the world. Many people work tirelessly and endlessly to promote happiness. Let their labors bring forth the joy that must live within that person. Allow them to shine as an example to others who are unable to give of themselves. Teach all of us that it is in giving that we receive, loving that we are loved and our faith in You that shall bring us peace.

Diplomat

All glory and honor is Yours, O blessed Jesus
Christ. Allow us to be Your diplomats of
peace. Place us where we can best do Your
work. Allow us to touch the lives of those that
have lost hope and give us the wisdom to see
answers that have eluded us. Establish a
sense of urgency in all people to find an end
to war and killing. Strengthen our resolve to
see You in all people and help us to rely more
closely on the power of prayer. Increase our
faith in Your promises so that we may have
the courage to ask for the blessings that You
offer.

Eye for an Eye

Change me, O God and renew my energy to pray, work and live for peace. Present new opportunities to all of us so that we may open dialogue and find new policies that will lead to a true and lasting peace. The evils of war are unspeakable and lasting for many generations. We still deeply mourn the many lives that were lost in our past wars and conflicts. Truly, an eye for an eye leaves the whole world blind. Open our minds, provide us with guidance, and allow us to find a way to live in peace.

The Vessel

O Jesus Christ, You are the strength that
sustains us. You have blessed us with the
wonderful gift of life. This gift is the vessel in
which we store and pour out the ingredients
that together make life sacred. Fill our vessel
with peace, love, hope, faith, generosity,
commitment, honesty, mercy, compassion,
fortitude, happiness and pureness of heart,
so that we may truly emulate You, O Jesus
Christ. Prevent us from making room for
sadness, envy, fear, hate, laziness, prejudice,
guilt, revenge, anger or sin, all of which
increases our separateness from You. Allow
peace to flow from every vessel until the
universe knows no war.

World's Potential

O Jesus Christ, You are the provider of all that we need. Bring peace and prosperity to all nations, especially those who live on the brink of poverty. Teach all of us to live in harmony and allow us to distribute our resources in a more evenly manner. Break down the walls of ethnic, religious and racial boundaries and make it possible for us to reach our true potential as Your children. May we all work toward the common goal of enriching the lives of all that have been given the gift of life.

The Glue

Dear Jesus Christ, You are the adhesive that holds the world together. Bring peace to those who suffer from broken relationships. Allow forgiveness to triumph over hurt and pain. Mend our broken hearts and give us the courage to offer a hand of reconciliation to those whom we deeply love. Allow the bitterness that we feel to be washed away and restore our trust. It is the respect that we show for those most difficult to love that is pleasing to You. Especially, bring the peace that You alone offer to families that have lost their loving bond.

Forgive Us

O Merciful God, You are our salvation. Bring peace to those who are unable to forgive. Free them from the pain that they have experienced. Show us how to forgive ourselves for the mistakes that we have made. May we experience forgiveness from those whom we have betrayed. Guide us to the path that You have laid before us and allow Your message of love to be heard.

Chapter VII

With
Every
Step
I
Take

Show Us God

Show the people on this earth how to live amongst themselves in love and peace. We are disobedient children in need of parental guidance and discipline. Please show Your grace and mercy and spare Your children of the disasters that are befalling us now. Forgive us of our transgressions against You and the planet You gave to us. Remove from us our negativity and all that is not pure within us. Cleanse us with Your healing light and continue to accept us as we are. Amen

Eternal Moment

You see into our hearts and hear our every prayer, dear Jesus Christ. End the silence that keeps us from healing, growing and becoming healthy. Allow us to forgive and to move forward on the path that leads to Your love. Nurture peace where it is most scarce and provide us with hope when darkness prevails. Shine the light of Your truth on the misconceptions that we have come to rely upon. Deliver us from our ability to take this life for granted and challenge us to live as Your children, keenly aware of the brevity of our earthly existence.

Atonement

Your mercy is without end, dear Jesus Christ. Allow our suffering to be atonement for the times that we have offended You. For the times that we ignored Your presence and when we refused Your help, we are sorry. Forgive us for the times we did not lend a hand to someone in need. Pardon us for our arrogance and for allowing injustice to live, while we busied ourselves with meaningless task. Teach us to see You in all people and to be ever aware of Your constant presence. Bring peace to our world, especially in places where war is most imminent.

Behold God

Behold God, to whom I look for eternal peace. May I please You in how I choose to live my life. Grant unto me, O God, the wisdom to know right from wrong, the courage to fight for the defenseless, and an open heart, so that I may be able to love those I now fear. Free me from the burden of vengeance, judgment and retribution so that I may find room for hope and forgiveness. Your peace is the treasure I seek.

Brokenness

In You, Jesus Christ, we are whole. Mend those who have been broken by the weight of self-doubt, feelings of inadequacy and guilt. Allow us to accept Your love and forgiveness and permit us to love ourselves. Give us the courage to reveal our talents and the wisdom to share them where they may best serve You. Renew our belief that peace is possible and will become evident when we learn to forgive and allow ourselves to love.

Chains

O Jesus Christ, You have given us the freedom to follow You or to turn away. Bring peace to those people who have made tragic mistakes with their lives. Have mercy on those who will spend their lives in prison and in the custody of others. Bring relief to the victims of crime and allow them to rise above their pain, hurt and fear. Be with children who live with foster families while their parents serve time incarcerated. Teach us all to live according to Your word and let those who have offended You come to know the depth of Your forgiveness. Free us from the chains of loneliness, insecurity, jealousy and depression and keep us ever aware of Your presence.

Chronic Pain

Dear God, we find great comfort and healing
through You. Provide peace to those that live
with chronic pain. Ease the suffering of those
with muscle, bone and joint pain. Relieve the
stress caused by disease and injury. Allow our
bodies to be renewed in health and provide
healing to those that have lost hope. Provide
us with patience as we deal with the torment
of physical ailments. Allow our suffering to
atone for the sins of those who bring sadness
to the world.

Defrost

O loving Jesus Christ, hear our unending praise and worship. Grant that we may live our lives so that we may one day be worthy to abide in Your direct presence. Keep us faithful to Your command to love one another. Teach us to search for peace where all hope has been lost. Give us the courage to select our political leaders from those who will find peaceful solutions to our problems while working for justice and respecting all life. Forgive those who do not follow You and keep us safe from their violent intentions. Bring dignity to all those who feel abandoned by You and society. Warm the hearts of those who have turned away from You so that they too may celebrate all that You offer.

Financial Peace

Great Provider, how wondrous are Your mighty deeds. I have been blessed with more than anyone could ever hope. Please provide financial peace to those that are burdened and are unable to enjoy their lives. Give them peace and allow them to find an honorable way out of their misery. Show them the joy of a simple life and keep them free from the slavery of materialism. As children, we make mistakes. Through Your divine intervention we are able to return to the path that leads to Your eternal salvation and happiness. Peace is found in You alone.

Our Potential

As Your children God, You have given us the potential to overcome all evil. Bring peace to those who turned away from You, but now realize the wrongs that they committed. Comfort those who are imprisoned and bless the victims of all crime. Ease the pain of regret for those who allowed selfishness, immaturity and fear to permit irreversible mistakes to be made. Open all of our hearts to forgiveness and keep us from judging others. Allow us to reach our potential so that our lives will honor You.

Remorse

Come down upon us, O God, and deliver us from our sadness. Forgive us for the mistakes that we have made and for the deeds that have added pain to our brothers and sisters. We are sorry for the actions that we did not take to ease the burden of someone that we did not know. We grieve for how we have accepted the plight of those living in poverty and famine. Guide us to live by Your law of love and give us the wisdom to live our lives so that we may one day be ready to live in Your presence. Thank You for Your love and for the gift of peace.

Steppingstones

You are my strength and my life, O God. May I never be without Your protection and love. Bless those who fight incurable disease and illness and bring peace into their lives. Offer them the gift of hope. Reach out to those who have denied You and show them Your unconditional love. Heal their broken bodies and fill each heart with the comfort of Your presence. Allow us to accept the challenges that have been placed before us as the steppingstones that lead to You.

Search for Peace

I am searching God for that which I do not know. I have everything that I ever sought and yet I am not whole. Fill my life with meaning and provide me with purpose. Allow me to do more than to go through the motions of life. Open my mind to a new beginning so that I may honor You through service. Open my heart to those I do not trust so that I may honor You through love. Alter my coarse and put me on the path that leads to peace.

Influence

Fill us with Your love, O Jesus Christ. Where there is fear, bring security. Where there is hatred, bring understanding. And, where there is sorrow, bring Your compassion. Allow Your peace to be known by all people and keep us mindful of our need to forgive. Bless those who have lost hope in You and renew our faith in Your mercy. Increase our desire to serve You and allow our actions to become the influence that leads to peace.

New Year's Day

Dear Jesus Christ, Thank You for bringing us to the dawn of a new year. Thank You for the protection, comfort and security that You provided during the past year. Allow us to live our lives, during the next year, free of worry and committed to doing Your will. We are confident that You will be with us during every laugh, tear and joy that life affords us and we depend upon You for direction and guidance. Allow us to use this year to make things better in our world, for ourselves and for the many generations that will inherit what we leave behind. Bless all of us with the peace that only You can give.

Anticipation

O Jesus Christ, You provide all that we need. Through Your love we are nourished and made whole. Give us a clear awareness of our potential and push us to use it in ways that help others. Teach us to reach out to those who seem untouchable. Establish peace in our hearts and allow it to radiate throughout our communities and world as we wait in hopeful anticipation of joining You in Eternity.

Chapter VIII

Take
And
Live
Each
Moment

191

Needless Anxiety

In You, O God, I place my trust. I shall not worry, for You are with me. Have You not protected me from the moment of my conception? I have not a moment to waste on needless anxiety, for You have blessed me with life and with hope. I shall work to replace all negative thoughts with acts of kindness. Allow me to become the person that You created for this world and give me the courage to accept Your challenges. Permit me to promote the message of peace, especially to those who do not know You.

Rest

You are our comfort, O Jesus Christ. Bring peace to those who have spent their energy celebrating Your love during the holiday season. Allow us to take the time to savor the kindness that people brought to one another. Let us enjoy the gifts that we shared and may the time that we offered helping others lead to long lasting reward. See in our hearts the burning love that we have for You, Jesus Christ. Allow us to see you in all those that we encounter.

Searching

All powerful and ever loving God, You know all my needs before I am aware of them. I struggle through life always searching for something different. When I was young, I dreamt of being old. When I became old, I yearned for my youth. I worry endlessly about my physical appearance and sacrifice my health to achieve little. My prayers are often a request to add to my riches and then I am burdened by the responsibilities that come with them. I scream for peace and quiet and yet I suffer great loneliness. Provide me with Your love so that I may enjoy what I have, share what I can offer and live in Your eternal peace. Bless those that are left searching for that which they do not know.

Just Me

Have mercy on us God and bless us with forgiveness and peace. Help us to overcome the hypocrisy that enables us to praise and not obey, worship and not be able to forgive, and hate without being able to find room for love. Remove the stress that governs our thoughts. Keep us close so that we may love and depend upon You for all things. Increase the vision that will allow us to see our enemy as our friend. Finally, make us aware that we are here for today only. In a moment our life may change. May we cherish and understand that this moment may be our last. Please provide peace so that we may accept the plan that You have for our lives. With You God, all things are possible.

Your Goodness

Your goodness feeds us, O God, and Your love is never ending. Keep us aware that Good will always win over evil. Alleviate all unnecessary anxiety as we place our concerns in Your hands. We realize that we must know sorrow in order to know joy, we must feel pain to recognize love and we must overcome fear to live in peace. Choose me to be Your humble servant and direct all of Your children to recognize the cherished gift of life.

We are Waiting

Dear God, smile upon those who have put their lives on hold. Let us end this waiting game that we think will take our lives in the direction we want. Remind us that our lives will go in the direction that You have designed for us. We wait for houses to sell, businesses to start, holidays to pass and people to die. We wait for weight loss, more money and the lottery. We wait for war and terrorism to stop while we anticipate the start of battle. If we could live for today, without wasting it on the worry of tomorrow, then perhaps, that would be peace. Show us Your peace and bless us with the gift of living in the moment.

Life with God

Hello God, Friend and Protector. If today is the last that I will spend here on Earth, allow me to live it in peace. Provide the wisdom to leave all worry up to You. Keep me from wasting a moment on things that I cannot control. Place Your emphasis on the people that I love and those that love me. Shield me from thinking negative thoughts or fearing what I do not understand. Stay close to me and allow me to love You as never before. Understand the gratitude that I have for the wonderful gift of life and regardless of when that gift ends, know that in You, I have lived.

Never Too Late

O God, You have revealed Your love to us and that has brought us peace. Provide an invitation to those individuals who feel it is too late to come to know You. Show them that the peace You offer is available to all Your children, regardless of age. From the moment of our creation, until our dying day, You welcome us into Your family. Stop anyone from missing the opportunity to live fully in Your love. Allow those blessed with faith to provide witness to Your greatness.

Living Prayer

Open our hearts to You, O God, and gather Your children in. Renew our hearts with peace and allow us to surrender ourselves to You. Keep our faith fresh and alive. Prevent us from merely going through the motions to get through life. Teach us to live our lives as a living prayer that honors You. May all that we do and all that we offer be for Your greater glory. Allow the peace that You have bestowed upon us to spread throughout the world.

Aspiration

True and perfect love comes from You, Jesus
Christ. Grant that we may foster peace in our
homes and in the lives of others. Teach us to
accept each new day as a mission to add
happiness to the world in which we live. Do
not allow us to take for granted one more
breath, for it may be our last. Challenge us to
utilize our talents so that we may realize the
best life that we can possibly live. Prepare
our hearts to be merciful toward those who
wish us harm and grant us the wisdom to
accept the challenges before us. May we all
grow in common unity, determined to love one
another as You have loved us. Bless all of
Your children with the aspiration to know You.

Chapter IX

In
Peace
Eternally

Dying

Your compassion is without end, O Jesus
Christ. Welcome into Your kingdom those
who are about to die. Accept them with the
love that You have shown to all of us and
bless them with Your mercy. May their new
Home be filled with unending peace and never
shall they know pain again. Remain close to
those who survive in this world and continue
to strengthen our faith in Your promises.
Allow me to be worthy of the place You have
designated for me when You choose to invite
me Home.

Eternal Peace

Divine and loving God, I come to You in time of great pain and fear. Cancer is consuming the life of someone I love. Provide them with comfort and watch over my family as we grieve. Be near to us all as we face the challenges that await us. If it is Your will and my loved one is most ready to enter into Your eternal kingdom, then bless our remaining time with peace. Fill us with faith and hope. Allow our acceptance of this part of life to stand as a testament to all those who fear death. Ease our pain and free us from the sadness that prevents us from living. Through conception we are born into life and through death we are born into eternal peace. Accept all of us into Your kingdom.

Passing

Bring peace to my loved one dear God as the end of their life nears. Comfort them as they make their way home to You. Death is the door to true peace with You and yet we approach it with fear. Wipe away all sorrow and bless us with the courage to face this part of our journey. Forgive Your child of any wrongs that they may have committed. Although I grieve the loss of my friend, I hand them over to You where they shall live with no more tears, absence of suffering and true peace. I long for the day that I too shall join You in Eternity.

Loss of a Child

We place our trust in You, Jesus Christ, for Your love is everlasting. Bring peace to our family and friends as we grieve. End our unceasing question of "why?" with the acceptance of knowing that Your ways are not our ways. Keep us mindful that each of Your children is created uniquely for one purpose and returns to You when they are most spiritually prepared to enter into Eternity. Allow us to be more like You in the blindness that You display toward our weaknesses and mistakes because Your love is both perfect and complete. Do not allow us to follow the false prophets of guilt, anger, depression or denial, which increases our distance from You and our beloved. Although we long for the day when we are reunited in Eternity, we thank You for the wonderful blessing that You brought into our lives.

In Memory

Everlasting God, You alone know our every need. How wonderful it is to be part of Your infinite plan. Please grant peace to those that have passed from this world. May they know the sweet blessings of Your kingdom. Have mercy on those that did not follow Your commandments. Let my suffering be an offering for those that have been unable to accept Your unconditional love. Help the non-believer to turn from their sad and unfulfilling path, to a road rich in the treasures that You have promised. Allow all caregivers to find peace and remind them that what they have done for their brother they have done for You. We look forward to the day that we join our loved ones and You in Your Eternal Kingdom of Love. Amen.

Unbearable Loss

You are with me always, Jesus Christ. Let me
see You when You seem so far away. Bring
peace to my heart as I question why such
sadness could be allowed into my life. Bring
comfort to my family and friends as we deal
with our tremendous loss. Keep our faith
strong in Your promises and let us
understand that You call each of us when we
are best prepared to join You in Eternity.
Have mercy on those who grieve and embrace
them with compassion. May all Your children
who leave this life enter into Your kingdom
without delay so that we may enjoy true peace
and the end of all sorrow. Please allow my
family the blessed comfort of knowing that
You have a plan far greater than what we are
able to see. Teach us to accept that pure
love sometimes blinds us from seeing or
understanding Your divine will. Bless us and
all of Your children with the gift of forgiveness

for words unspoken, deeds undone and remove the guilt that keeps us from growing closer to You. Welcome each of us into Your sacred presence and accept our eternal gratitude for allowing us to have shared Your precious gift of our loved one.

Amen

Let there be peace on earth
And
Let it begin with me

John T. Mudd
April 11, 1964 – December 9, 2008

The
Beginning

Photo Credits

All of the photos in this book were either taken by John, of John, or are directly related to John.

Chapter I photo is taken from the bluff that overlooks "The Burg" where John's parents live.

Chapter II photo is of John's original *Gift of Peace* book.

Chapter III photo is of John's cabin decorated for Christmas, two nights before the fire.

Chapter IV is a photo taken of *The Creation* painting that was in John's kitchen. It was one of the first pieces of artwork he ever bought. It too, was well traveled.

Chapter V photo is taken of a painting that was in John's cabin.

Chapter VI photo is of the waterfall on his parent's farm.

Chapter VII photo is also taken on the family farm. It is John's nephew, giving his niece a lift.

Chapter VIII photo was taken at John's grandfather's home where the family gathered for Papaw's 93rd birthday. John appears to be completely captivating the grandchildren. This probably has a little to do with his amazing story telling abilities, and a lot to do with the fact that they are all sitting in the bathtub.

Chapter IX photo was taken by John. There was a dead tree on the land adjoining his parent's farm where he hoped to someday build a home. This tree was his very favorite. He saw so much beauty in it, as he did most things that were sometimes difficult for others to see.

The last photo is taken of John standing in his yard. Although we can no longer see his face, we are eternally grateful that we can still hear his voice.

INDEX

Made in the USA
Charleston, SC
20 October 2011